DUE DATE	**BRODART**	**07/95**	**14.95**

American Events

THE ORPHAN TRAINS

Annette R. Fry

New Discovery Books
New York

Maxwell Macmillan Canada
Toronto

Maxwell Macmillan International
New York Oxford Singapore Sydney

Book design: Deborah Fillion
Cover photo courtesy of Kansas State Historical Society

New Discovery Books
Macmillan Publishing Company
866 Third Avenue
New York, NY 10022

Maxwell Macmillan Canada, Inc.
1200 Eglinton Avenue East
Suite 200
Don Mills, Ontario M3C 3N1

Macmillan Publishing Company is part of the Maxwell Communication
Group of Companies.

First Edition

Printed in the United States of America

10 9 8 7 6 5 4 3 2 1

Library of Congress Cataloging-in-Publication Data

Fry, Annette R.
        The orphan trains / by Annette R. Fry
            p.   cm. — (American events)
        Includes bibliographical references and index.
        ISBN 0-02-735721-X
        1. Orphan trains—Juvenile literature. [1. Orphan trains.
    2. Orphans.] I. Title. II. Series.
        HV985.F79 1994
        362.7′34′0973—dc20   93-37933
Summary: An examination of the placing out of orphaned, poor, and abandoned children from eastern cities such as New York and Boston to homes
in the West, begun by the Children's Aid Society.

CONTENTS

WANTED
HOMES for CHILDREN

A company of homeless children from the East will arrive at

TROY, MO., ON FRIDAY, FEB. 25th, 1910

These children are of various ages and of both sexes, having been thrown friendless upon the world. They come under the auspices of the Childern's Aid Society of New York. They are well disciplined, having come from the various orphanages. The citizens of this community are asked to assist the agent in finding good homes for them. Persons taking these children must be recommended by the local committee. They must treat the children in every way as a member of the family, sending them to school, church, Sabbath school and properly clothe them until they are 17 years old. The following well-known citizens have agreed to act as local committee to aid the agents in securing homes:

O. H. AVERY E. B. WOOLFOLK H. F. CHILDERS
WM. YOUNG   G. W. COLBERT

Applications must be made to, and endorsed by, the local committee.

An address will be made by the agent. Come and see the children and hear the address. Distribution will take place at the

Opera House, Friday,
Feb. 25, at 1:30 p. m.

B. W. TICE and MISS A. L. HILL, Agents, 105 E. 22nd St., New York City. Rev. J. W. SWAN, University Place, Nebraska, Western Agent.

A newspaper ad announces the arrival of one of the many orphan trains that brought children from eastern cities to new homes in the West.

Chapter 1

WHAT TO DO WITH THE CHILDREN?

The problem of unwanted children has always haunted society.

In ancient times one solution to the problem was a practice known as exposure—leaving a baby out in the cold to die or to be found by someone who might want a child. Exposure of babies is a practice that has never stopped. In the 19th century people referred to this as abandonment rather than exposure. Sometimes the unwanted infant would be wrapped up warmly and left in a basket on the steps of a church or at the door of a house. Whatever their condition or wherever they were found, abandoned babies were known as foundlings.

One hundred and fifty years ago in New York City, hardly a day passed without the discovery of an abandoned baby. It might have been left on a doorstep or put with the trash in a back alley. Of course, in those days modern methods of birth control were unknown. As for abortion, it all too often resulted in the death of the mother.

In 19th-century America there were other, less drastic ways of solving the problem of superfluous children. Especially the offspring of the very poor. One method was called a vendue.

In a vendue impoverished families were auctioned off by the town fathers. The *lowest* bidder got the family. The town gave the bid-

A mother places her baby in a receptacle built to house abandoned children until they could be safely rescued.

A group of street children appear before the New York City commissioners of charity.

der the sum of money he'd named. It was then up to him to stretch the money to feed and house the family for a year. What he got out of the arrangement was a form of slave labor. The people in his charge—children included—became his unpaid employees. In some localities of the northeastern United States, auctioning off poor people took the place of public aid as late as the 1850s.

The idea that government should help poor families stay together in their own homes was not a popular one. The nearest thing to helping keep a family together was something called outdoor relief. Outdoor relief provided charity handouts for destitute mothers. These usually took the form of baskets of food and meager allowances for fuel and children's clothes.

What public officials preferred was to herd all the down-and-outs of the community into big institutions. These went by various names: almshouse, poorhouse, poor farm, county farm, workhouse. In most of these places living conditions were appalling. Children were thrust among adults of every kind, including the diseased, the senile, and the mentally ill. A New York State commission reported:

> The great mass of poor houses are most disgraceful memorials of the public charity. Common domestic animals are usually more humanely provided for than the paupers in some of these institutions.[1]

Gradually, concerned people began to realize that children should be removed from such crowded and dangerous places. Children, after all, have different needs than adults. The private orphan asylum began to replace the poorhouse as a home for orphaned and abandoned children.

But, before long, even the new orphan asylums weren't enough to take care of the growing hordes of destitute children in cities like New York.

New York was in a period of frenzied growth, with immigrants from Europe pouring in at the rate of 1,000 a day.[2] Most were from Germany and Ireland.

In the overcrowded slums disease took a frightful toll, especially on the children. The big killer was tuberculosis, and it was always present. There were also epidemics of cholera, yellow fever, typhus, and other infections that thrive in unsanitary conditions.

Children who had somehow managed to survive often lost their parents. This could mean they were left on their own. Other children were on their own because they ran away when life at home became intolerable. Child abuse and alcoholism were rampant.

New York became filled with homeless and delinquent children.

At the time when the city's population was around 500,000, the police estimated that there were 10,000 boys and girls living on the streets.[3]

The vagrant children—street arabs, they were called then—slept where they could: in doorways and cellars, under stairways, in outhouses (privies), on hay barges, and in discarded packing boxes. Some of them earned a few pennies a day by selling newspapers, matches, rags from the dump heaps, and coal picked up piece by piece on streets and wharves. Others survived by begging and stealing.

The older boys often became members of street gangs that terrified respectable citizens when they weren't bashing one another's heads in. And many of the girls were experienced prostitutes by the time they were 12 years old.

In 1849 New York City's chief of police sounded the alarm about the "constantly increasing number of vagrant, idle and vicious children of both sexes, who infest our public thoroughfares, hotels, and docks."[4]

The respectable citizens of New York were horrified and fearful. Suddenly, the situation seemed to have grown out of hand. They were even more horrified a short time later by a grand jury report on serious crimes:

> Of the higher grades of felony, four-fifths of the complaints examined have been against minors. And two-thirds of all complaints acted on during the term have been against persons between the ages of 19 and 21.[5]

Clearly, something had to be done about the growing ranks of young people like these, something to keep children who were not yet juvenile delinquents from the temptations of crime, something that would keep them from growing up ignorant and unskilled in an overcrowded city, something to prevent them from becoming costly burdens on society.

Chapter 2

MR. BRACE COMES UP
WITH A SOLUTION

I n 1852 a young clergyman, the Reverend Charles Loring Brace, began a career as a missionary. His mission was to a society as foreign to him and his New England forebears as any in Asia or Africa. It was a mission among the people he called "the dangerous classes."

And dangerous they were. For Mr. Brace's work took him not only to the prison on New York City's Blackwells Island (today called Roosevelt Island). It also took him to the sinister Five Points district on the Lower East Side. In the Five Points, it was said, no human life was safe.

Most of the buildings in the jam-packed city slums were tenements. In a typical tenement several families might share an apartment. Water had to be carried upstairs from a pump in the backyard. And the only toilets were outdoor privies.

Mr. Brace soon despaired of his efforts to improve the lot of families living like that. But what struck him most was the very same thing that concerned the police: the children. He was appalled by the "immense number of boys and girls floating and drifting about our streets, with hardly any assignable home or occupation, who continually swelled the multitude of criminals, prostitutes and vagrants."[1]

The 25-year-old urban missionary was ready to give up on the

The crowded tenements of New York's Lower East Side, where many of the children who went West on the orphan trains came from.

Annette R. Fry

The Reverend Charles Loring Brace, founder of the Children's Aid Society

adults. But not on the children. Adults might be beyond reform. But there was hope, he believed, for the "neglected youth" and "little waifs of society who, through no fault of their own, were cast out on the currents of a large city."[2]

Mr. Brace was determined to save the children by getting them off the streets, then helping them to become useful members of society. He was convinced that big, impersonal, regimented institutions were not good places for children to live. He maintained that state reform schools and city prisons, juvenile asylums and "houses of refuge" for potential delinquents, as well as foundling hospitals and orphan asylums could be deadly to both body and mind.

In the foundling hospital run by the city nine out of ten of the illegitimate and abandoned babies died. "The truth seems to be," the young clergyman observed, "that each infant needs one nurse or caretaker, and that if you place these delicate creatures in large companies together in any public building, an immense proportion are sure to die."[3]

All those new asylums—public and private—added up to "a bad preparation for practical life," in Mr. Brace's opinion. "The child, most of all, needs individual care and sympathy. In an asylum, he is 'Letter B, of Class 3,' or 'No. 2, of Cell 426,' and that is all that is known of him.…And, what is very natural, *the longer he is in the asylum, the less likely he is to do well in outside life.*"[4]

In a series of newspaper articles, the young reformer outlined the problems. The solutions he proposed were based on three main principles: useful work, education both practical and religious, and a homelike environment among caring adults. If those simple principles were followed, he predicted, there would be less crime. And the city would be relieved of overcrowding.

Mr. Brace called for a new kind of organization to carry out his ideas. It would be devoted entirely to the needs of poor and homeless children. The result was the founding of the Children's Aid Society of New York in March of 1853. Though Mr. Brace still hoped to become a minister with a parish, he agreed to run the new organization for a year at a salary of $1,000. He ended by staying with the society for the rest of his life.

The first thing the new society did was to announce how it proposed to save the children who swarmed the city streets. There would be lodging houses, reading rooms, and schools where both boys and girls could learn trades. There would also be a network of employment opportunities suitable for their years:

> We hope especially to be the means of draining the city of these children, by communicating with farmers, manufacturers, or families in the country, who may have need of such for employment. When homeless boys are found by our agents, we mean to get them homes in the families of respectable, needy persons in the city, and put them in the way of an honest living.[5]

Self-help rather than charity handouts was stressed. The Aid Society would "give education and work rather than alms" so that those they aided "will never need either private or public charity."[6]

The news quickly spread among the city's outcast children. Mr. Brace described their reaction in one of his books, *The Dangerous Classes of New York, and Twenty Years' Work among Them:*

> Most touching of all was the crowd of wandering little ones who immediately found their way to the office. Ragged young girls who had nowhere to lay their heads; children driven from drunkards' homes; orphans who slept where they could find a box or a stairway; boys cast out by step-mothers or step-fathers; newsboys, whose incessant answer to our question, "Where do you live?" rang in our ears, *"Don't live nowhere!"*; little bootblacks, young peddlers, "canal-boys" who seem to drift into the city every winter and live a vagabond life; pickpockets and petty thieves trying to get honest work; child beggars and flower-sellers growing up to enter courses of crime—all this motley throng of infantile misery and childish guilt passed through our doors, telling their simple stories of suffering, and loneliness, and temptation, until our hearts became sick.[7]

Mr. Brace's belief in useful work was reflected in all of the activities of the new society. The newsboys' lodging house offered a bed, a bath, and a hot meal for pennies a day to the hardworking juvenile salesmen. (The payment rule was designed to insure habits of thrift among the youthful entrepreneurs.) The workshops—vocational schools for girls as well as boys—provided services that simply weren't available in the city schools. So, too, did the Aid Society's reading rooms and night schools. And they did this in neighborhoods where many children had never been inside a schoolroom. Clothes, shoes, and hot lunches were also provided.

The idea that even small children should learn practical work

The Bettmann Archive

Some of the many street children that the Children's Aid Society helped become newsboys.

skills was a popular one. Americans took it for granted that most children would earn their keep by working. It was a rare family who could afford to let their children have more than a few years of school. Working children were *needed*. Ever since the coming of the first settlers, there had been a labor shortage in America. There were never enough hands to chop down trees, build houses and roads, farm the land, make clothes, prepare the food, take care of the babies. Children performed all these tasks, and more. With the growth of industry they also helped earn money for the family by working in mills and factories.

On farms and in factories the working day for children could be as long as 10 or 12 hours. The wages in the factories were pitiful: 25 to 50 cents a day.[8] In families where there were too many mouths to feed, parents sent their sons and daughters to be "bound out" as indentured workers. Indenture was a legal contract that bound one person to work for another for a certain length of time *without pay.* Public poorhouses and private orphan asylums also relieved their overcrowding by indenturing. Even little girls were sent out to be indentured servants.

When the Children's Aid Society was founded, indenture kept many young people off the streets and out of institutions—which was exactly what Mr. Brace also wanted to do. But he disapproved of indenture. And he wanted to make sure that children were put in *good homes*—good "Christian homes" where they could help the family and also be part of the family.

The disadvantage of indenture, in the clergyman's opinion, was that it was too rigid an arrangement. Under his plan, children would go to homes where they'd be expected to share the work of the family. No formal agreements would tie them down. They would be *placed* out, not *bound* out.

In addition to placing children with families, Mr. Brace proposed finding paying jobs for teenagers.

If a family or employer was unhappy with someone provided by the society, or that someone was unhappy with them, the arrangement could be ended. The young person remained the society's responsibility, and the society would find him or her another home or job. On the other hand, if all went well and a family wanted to adopt the child, they could do so.

A few children were soon placed with families in the city, while jobs were found for the older boys. But getting them far, far away from the crime and squalor of city slums was what Mr. Brace wanted most to do. "The best of all asylums for the outcast child," he wrote, "is the *farmer's home.*"

On the farms of America at that time, the demand for labor was never ending. As Mr. Brace saw it, it was a simple case of supply and demand. And his organization had the supply. Also, as he pointed out, the farm families who wanted help didn't want servants. They wanted young people who would be members of the family.

"With their overflowing supply of food, each new mouth in the household brings no drain on their means. Children are a blessing, and the mere feeding of a young boy or girl is not considered at all."[9]

By the end of its first year, the Children's Aid Society could report: "We have thus far sent off to homes in the country, or to places where they could earn an honest living, 164 boys and 43 girls, of whom some 20 were taken from prison, where they had been placed for being homeless in the streets."[10]

All of these were individual placements in New York and nearby states. With more and more youngsters coming to the doors of the society, the next step was *group* placements. Now the children would go to more distant states: to towns and villages in the great American heartland where there was an unlimited demand for healthy young folk to help on the farms.

In September of 1854 the dream of new homes in the rural West for city children became a reality. What was later to be called an orphan train arrived in a small town in southwest Michigan.

It was the first of many. During the next 75 years, the orphan trains took children from American cities to towns from Maine to Florida, from Virginia to California. It was a migration of children unique in human history.

There were 46 of them in the first group of "little emigrants" from the city. They were almost entirely boys, ranging in age from 7 to

15, and they were under the charge of a youthful agent of the society, the Reverend E. P. Smith.

The plan was to go by riverboat—the *Isaac Newton*—from New York City to Albany, then by train to Buffalo, then by lake steamer to Detroit, and onto another train for the final lap of their journey to the village of Dowagiac, Michigan.

As Mr. Smith told the story, his charges were wearing their first clean clothes in years and were in high spirits. The passengers were so taken with the stories told by the former "street rats" that two of them took boys then and there.

At Albany the train station was jammed with others who were also headed West. Hundreds of newcomers to the United States filled the platforms. They were German, Irish, Italian, and Norwegian. Like the emigrant youngsters in Mr. Smith's group, the immigrant families were hopeful of new and happier lives at the end of their journey.

Smith and his charges now boarded a train for Buffalo. The car they traveled in all night long was hot and crowded. There were no lights and little sleep to be had on the rough benches. But the morning brought unexpected sights.

They were now passing through the countryside of upstate New York. Many of the boys had never seen a farm. They gazed in awe at the cows, the apple orchards, and the fields of corn.

Going from one end of Lake Erie to the other by boat was the longest part of the journey. Sleeping on the boat from Buffalo to Detroit was a bit of a problem, what with "a touch of seasickness, and of the stamping, neighing, and the bleating of a hundred horses and sheep over our heads."

At ten o'clock on Saturday night, they landed in Detroit. The now rumpled and dirty band of street kids once more got on a train. When they arrived at their final destination, it was three o'clock in the morning. It was too late to do anything except stretch out on the station floor for a few hours of sleep.

Refreshed by a big breakfast and a washup at the local hotel, the youthful group astonished the villagers by filing into the little church. At the end of the sermon, the minister invited Mr. Smith to explain the purpose of their visit. The congregation immediately expressed interest.

The following morning "the boys held themselves in readiness to receive applications from the farmers. They would watch in all directions, scanning closely every wagon that came in sight, and deciding from the appearance of the driver and the horses, more often from the latter, whether they 'would go in for *that* farmer.'

"There seems to be a general dearth of boys," continued Mr. Smith in his report, "and a still greater of girls in all this section. Before night I had applications for fifteen of my children, the applicants bringing recommendations from their pastor and the justice of peace.

"There was a rivalry among the boys to see which first could get a home in the country, and before Saturday they were all gone....

"On the whole, the first experiment of sending children West is a very happy one, and I am sure there are places enough with good families in Michigan, Illinois, Iowa, and Wisconsin, to give every poor boy and girl in New York a permanent home. The only difficulty is to bring the children to the homes."[11]

In the years to come the Children's Aid Society developed smoothly run procedures for finding homes in the country for some 100,000 young people. Other child-saving organizations (as they were called then) followed the society's lead with their own orphan trains.

At the same time, the Aid Society set up many other programs for disadvantaged city children—programs that continue to this day.

But the real story of the orphan train movement is not one of organizations and procedures. It is the story of the individual children who made those journeys into the unknown.

An engraving depicts the story of children taken from the city streets to new homes in the west.

Chapter 3

NEW HOMES
IN THE WEST

One day not long after the first orphan train set out from the city, a kindhearted New Yorker by the name of Slater befriended a bedraggled street urchin. With his thin cheeks and pale face, the boy had the look of a sad little old man.

After giving him a good breakfast, Mr. Slater took him to the offices of the Children's Aid Society. There he was gently questioned:

"Where are your father and mother, my boy?"

"Both dead, sir."

"Where are your other relatives and friends?"

"Hain't got no friends, sir. I live by myself on the street."

"Where did you stay?"

"Slept in the privy sometime, sir. And then in the stables in 16th street."

"Poor fellow," said someone, "how did you get your living?"

"Begged it. And then, them stablemen, they gave me bread sometimes."

"Have you ever been to school, or Sunday school?"

"No, sir."

A few days later, Mr. Slater's urchin was put with a group bound for new homes in Illinois. A note in the society's ledger tells briefly what happened to him:

"The lad was taken by an old gentleman of property, who, being childless, has since adopted him as his own, and will make him heir to a property."[1]

The boy was but one of thousands who came, or were brought, to the offices of the Children's Aid Society: newsboys and shoeshine boys wanting to go west to the land of cowboys and Indians; little match girls and flower sellers, ragged and barefoot; frowsy "bummers" who slept among the adult homeless on the floors of police stations; immigrant children who had somehow become separated from their families; boys and girls who had been living in the society's lodging houses.

But street arabs weren't the only ones who found their way to the society's door. There were the children brought in by desperate fathers or mothers. Among these unhappy parents were young women with babies and tales of desertion; workmen whose wives had died in childbirth; mothers with tuberculosis, far too ill to care for their families; and workwomen unable to cope with large broods.

Adding to the throng of westward-bound children were those turned over to the society by orphan asylums, or sent by the courts, or transferred from the huge public institutions on the islands of New York's East River.

Finally, there were the children brought in by concerned citizens like Mr. Slater.

These penniless, abandoned, orphan and half-orphan boys and girls soon set out on journeys they would remember for the rest of their lives. They traveled in groups of around 30 and 40, and sometimes many more, under the watchful care of agents of the society. One trainload bound for a Pennsylvania town in 1855 carried 138 children. This was an exceptionally large company. (As a rule boys outnumbered girls, but this group was made up of 72 girls and 66 boys.[2])

A journey to a midwestern state might take as long as a week. When trains reached the towns of their destination, the children were

A group of orphans, accompanied by Children's Aid Society representatives, arrives in Lebanon, Missouri.

welcomed by members of a local committee. These were prominent citizens who had made the preparations for their arrival. What happened next to these "companies of little emigrants" is described in Charles Loring Brace's *The Dangerous Classes:*

> The farming community having been duly notified, there was usually a dense crowd of people at the station, awaiting the arrival of the youthful travelers. The sight of the little company of the children of misfortune always touched the hearts of a population naturally generous. They were soon billeted around among the citizens, and the following day a public meeting was called in the church or town hall....
>
> The agent then addressed the assembly, stating the benevolent objects of the Society, and something of the history of the children. The sight of their worn faces was a most pathetic enforcement of his arguments. People who were childless came forward to adopt children. Others, who had not intended to take any into their families, were induced to apply for them. And many who really wanted the child's labor pressed forward to obtain it.[3]

Among a group of 40 children sent to Iowa in 1875 was a little Irish immigrant named Willie.

Four-year-old Willie had been brought to the office of the society by an officer of the Prison Association. The Prison Association was a group that concerned itself with the welfare of prisoners and their families.

To the western agent of the society, the boy was "a hard subject." He was mischievous, hyperactive, a regular hellion. A German couple were the only ones among the throng at the Grange Hall in the little midwestern town who considered taking Willie. "He please my old man," the farmer's wife explained as she carried him off.

Several months later the same agent stopped by the farm to see how Willie was getting on. The farmer was alarmed.

"Mr. Agent, if you come to take dot poy away, if you don't got de piggest yob on your hants what you never had, den I don't know how it is. I wouldn't take the whole United States for dot poy."

"I haven't come to take him away," the agent replied. "But how in the world do you manage him?"

"Oh, dot's easy," said the farmer's wife. "You see, we all luff him."

"This good woman had given us in one line the key to the success of the western work," the agent reported to the New York office. *"You see, we all love him.*

"There is an abundance of love and shelter and pity here that will never be exhausted. Send out the little ones in yet larger numbers. The work is a success!"[4]

By the 1870s the orphan trains of the Children's Aid Society were pulling into towns in more than 30 states. More than 3,000 children a year were finding new homes far from city slums. American-born children made up the biggest single group, followed by immigrant children from Germany and Ireland.[5]

During this period, the society's western agent was reporting travels of over 30,000 miles a year to check up on his charges. And the files of the society were full of letters from foster parents telling of happy adjustments.

"I have often had occasion to bless kind providence for having wafted to me a child of so fair promise, both as regards moral and mental excellence," enthused a man from Elkhart County, Indiana. "She has made good progress in her books, having advanced from her ABCs to McGuffey's Fourth Reader....My unbounded gratitude to the Children's Aid Society for having cast the dear one in my way."[6]

A girl from Indiana called the society "a blessing to mankind," and told how she loved to milk the cows and feed "the sweet little pigs." What she liked best of all was horseback riding. "I have ridden young horses and got thrown off twice, but it did not hurt me. They say I am a good girl but too wild and daring, and will get my neck broke if I do not stop; but I must have some fun."[7]

When the Civil War broke out, many of the older boys rushed to enlist with a regiment of society boys serving in the Union army. Many rose in the ranks to become officers. One young man, killed at the battle of Antietam, left a bequest of $100 to the "Children's Aid Society which has done so much for me."[8]

Annette R. Fry

Charles Fry, one of the first western agents of the Children's Aid Society and a relative of the author, went from town to town looking for good homes for the children the Society sent West.

Most of the older boys from New York City had to work for their keep. None of these arrangements were formal indentures, although the results were often pretty much the same. In 1870 one ex-newsboy in Illinois, now a grown man, told how he had left "a hard master" and found a good job with another farmer. He was hoping to move farther West to stake out his own 160 acres on the plains. (The famous Home-

Howard Darnell, one of the orphan train riders, with his adoptive parents shortly after his arrival in the West.

stead Act of 1862 provided free land to anyone who lived on it and farmed it for five years.)

"There is a good chance for a fellow out here," the former news-boy wrote. "I can plow, corn, and bind in the harvest, or anything in that line, and I can split rails first-rate....Be sure and try to get Jimmy out here. And if he ain't got any money, I will send him enough."[9]

In the minds of a lot of the transplanted New Yorkers, Iowa was as far away as California:

"The far West is a splendid country," reported J. P. from Tama County, Iowa, "a most luxurious country. Poverty is hardly known. What a blessing it is to me that I should come out. I am getting on well, let me tell you; very happy and comfortable; a good home and lots of true friends. I'm getting to be quite a Western farmer....I have $50 from summer work.

"The young lady who came out with us is still in the same place. They are all wanting girls out here, and they wish me to tell you so." The letter was signed, "I remain a thankful boy."[10]

As Mr. Brace had predicted, there was a tremendous demand for willing workers in the American heartland. Girls and young women were needed almost as much as youthful farmhands.

"Could you send about a dozen good *reliable* young German women to this place?" wrote "an influential lady of Ohio" in 1869. "They could all get work and do well. I have been without a girl four weeks, and sent 30 miles in a buggy to obtain one without success....I do not want a poor one, but would be willing to teach if good and worthy. My choice would be a good washer and ironer, and cook, of course." And then she adds: "I would take a Norwegian girl if one could be obtained."[11]

For hundreds of young people, taking jobs like these opened the door for a far better life than they could ever have found in the slums of New York City.

Despite the frequent happy endings, joining an orphan train to escape from city life was not always an easy thing for young people to do.

Little effort, apparently, was made to keep brothers and sisters together. Occasionally, more or less by chance, they were placed together or in the same neighborhood.

One rare case where siblings found homes close to each other

Jennie McDowell Davis

Jennie McDowell (in center wearing white bonnet) as she arrived on an orphan train in Missouri and (on facing page) with her adoptive sister, Bessie Holman. Her brother, Harry (on right marked with an X), was not so fortunate, moving from home to home.

was that of nine-year-old Wilhelmina and her sister, seven-year-old Dora. The two girls had been rescued from a cellar full of rats. They both bore scars from beatings at the hands of a drunken father. They were taken on the overnight Hudson River boat to upstate New York, where Wilhelmina was "adopted into the family of Dr. A.E.W. and the younger one...by a lady living next door.

"They are beautiful children," wrote the woman who had escorted them from the city. And she described how in the space of

Jennie McDowell Davis

three days they had "so engaged the sympathy and love of their future guardians as to render their presence quite indispensable.

"The new mothers, as the children call the two ladies, have spent most of the time since their arrival in making new clothes for them, and giving them all they can eat of the best food the country affords....

"The children are to go to school and keep their native German language, which they now speak very properly, and as soon as possible they will begin music."[12]

In the Children's Aid Society's first quarter of a century, a lot of changes had been going on in the United States.

During the 1850s, 2,600,000 newcomers entered the country. Most of them came from Ireland and Germany. At the same time, thousands of miles of railroad tracks were laid, and the railroads from the East were penetrating deep into the midwestern prairies.

During the 1860s, the Civil War tore the nation apart. The farms of the Midwest had to produce food as never before. And this at a time when many young men had gone off to fight. The war also made many orphans. As in many wars the rich grew richer and the poor grew poorer: In New York City the number of children in almshouses tripled.

In the next decade a financial panic led to a depression that continued throughout the 1870s. Thousands of businesses closed. Tens of thousands were out of work. In one three-month period in 1874, 90,000 homeless people slept in New York City police stations.[13]

And, in the 1870s, the Children's Aid Society shipped more children to farm homes than ever before or since. Meanwhile, a number of other groups had started to send out their own orphan trains. The Children's Aid Society now had competition.

Chapter 4

THE BABY TRAINS

he baby train is coming to town! The baby train is coming to town!" Babies and toddlers—by the dozens, by the carloads—were being greeted in town after town by families looking for little ones to fill a void.

They were foundling children, wards of the Foundling Asylum of the Sisters of Charity of Mount St. Vincent, on their way to new homes with Catholic families. Their destinations were towns in the Midwest and South where there were substantial Catholic communities.

The groups from the Foundling Asylum were considerably larger than the 30-some average of the Children's Aid Society. Generally, these baby contingents numbered around 50. However, one baby train that steamed into the Loreauville, Louisiana, station not long after the end of the 19th century carried 300 orphaned or abandoned little children. (Over the years Louisiana was the state that probably received the largest proportion of the New York babies.)[1]

Most of these little outcasts would not have lasted long in New York City. They were saved by an institution founded shortly after the Civil War.

Sister Irene Fitzgibbon was the founder and for many years the guiding light of the new Foundling Asylum. (In the 1890s the name "Hospital" replaced "Asylum.") One of her main objects in establishing the home for unwanted babies was to prevent infanticide—a crime that occurred almost every day in New York.

As soon as the new asylum opened its doors, Sister Irene had a white-curtained bassinet placed in the vestibule. Within the first month—a cold midwinter month—45 babies were left there during the night. Often as not, little notes had been pinned to the garments of these "waifs on the sea of sin," as one writer called them.

One note, addressed to the "Sisters of the House," told of a mother's love for her little Charley:

> Necessity compels me to part with my darling boy. I leave him hoping and trusting that you will take care of him. Will you let some kind-hearted lady adopt him as her own while he is young that he may never know but what she is his mother. God alone knows the bitter anguish of my heart in parting with this little dear. For God's sake remember the broken-hearted mother. Be good to my dear little Charley.[2]

Many newborns were in a pitiful condition by the time they arrived at the hospital: sickly, dehydrated, suffering from exposure. To provide them with the best infant nourishment in existence—mother's milk—a boarding-out department was launched. Married women were paid to nurse the newborns in their homes. These women were recent mothers. Either their own babies had died, or they had plenty of milk to spare while still nursing their own babies. Such women were called wet nurses.

Even with the boarding-out program, the Foundling Hospital was soon full to bursting. One winter night a young woman, scarcely more than a girl, showed up with her tiny baby. She begged the sisters for shelter for herself as well as her child.

Kindly but firmly, Sister Irene explained that they had no room for mothers.

The young mother came back again the next night, and was

Two Sisters of Charity record information about a foundling.

again refused. On the third night she added to her plea for shelter, "If you'll only let me stay here with my baby, then I can nurse another baby, too."

Sister Irene now realized that she was being presented with a sensible solution to a serious problem. Keeping mothers and children together would go a long way toward insuring the survival of the little ones in the perilous first six months. Thus began a program for providing asylum for mothers as well as babies—whether unmarried girls or needy married women who had been abandoned or widowed.[3]

A group of young orphan train riders smiles for a portrait.

The survival record of Sister Irene's babies was to make the New York Foundling Hospital world famous. Deaths from the killer diseases of the time—among them smallpox, diphtheria, and scarlet fever—were rare behind its doors. The sisters enforced the strictest isolation the moment a contagious disease was detected. And, though statistics are hard to come by, the kind of infant mortality Sister Irene most deplored—infanticide—appears to have drastically declined. In the 1890s a prominent social reformer pointed out that, thanks to the

Foundling Hospital, "Child murder has been practically stamped out in the city of New York."[4]

But there was still the problem of what to do with the children as they grew older. Until the children were three years old, they could be claimed by their parents. This was because poor families, as well as destitute and unwed mothers, sometimes left babies with the sisters hoping to be able to come for them someday. After three years of age, if still unclaimed, the foundling could be legally adopted by others. From time to time requests for adoptions came in from childless Catholic families in and around New York. But that still left a lot of growing children in a facility designed for babies.

The Children's Aid Society had already shown how placing its wards in free foster homes in the country, far from the temptations of the city, was a dramatically successful way of keeping dependent youngsters from becoming public burdens.

In the mid-1870s the Sisters of Charity followed the Aid Society's lead and embarked on their own placing-out program. They began with towns in Pennsylvania and Maryland and soon expanded their efforts to states farther West. The children they sent out were almost always toddlers and babies, and rarely more than five or six years of age.

The procedures determined by Sister Irene were quite different from those of Mr. Brace of the Aid Society. For the Foundling Asylum's little wards, there was to be no public display on the stage of a small-town opera house or meeting hall, no public rejection as the more attractive ones among them were the first to be chosen. Each and every boy and girl was spoken for in advance. Each bore a numbered tag with the names of his or her foster parents-to-be. And the designated parents, with names and numbers in hand, were waiting at the station to pick them up.

The quest for new homes and new families began when an agent scouted out Catholic communities in the Midwest and South in search

A group of little ones from the Foundling Asylum dressed in their best and carrying toys for their train trip West.

of places where small children might be welcomed. He would meet with the local pastors to find out if any of their parishioners would be interested in providing a home for a foundling. On Sunday morning the pastor would explain the program in church. Those who wanted to be foster parents would be given questionnaires to fill out. They could even describe the kind of child they wanted:

"Please send me a fair-complexioned little girl of three—blue

The crowded girls' dining room in the Foundling Asylum

eyes, light hair (not red), healthy and good looking."

"Your agent has promised me a nice red-haired boy. I have a red-haired wife and five red-headed girls and we want a boy to match."

"Send us a smart, stout, saucy boy of six, Irish parents."

"She *must* have a pretty nose," specified a prospective parent who put in an order for a "little brown-haired, blue-eyed girl."[5]

As with the Children's Aid Society, the agent also visited the homes where children were placed to see how things were going. In addition, the sisters who brought the children out personally checked up on the homes:

"We arrived safe with our twenty-five little charges," one sister wrote from Wisconsin, "to find their good foster papas and mamas awaiting our coming. We systematically gave out the children to the persons for whom they were destined except two, whose would-be parents, misunderstanding the time of our arrival, missed us. These little ones were quickly asked for by lookers-on who, it seemed, were nearly 1,000 in number."[6] The would-be parents apparently turned up the next day to claim their children.

The pastors who had children from the asylum in their congregations were also asked to check up on them each year. In general, their write-ups were favorable. Some 20 years after the program was launched, a Wisconsin pastor reported that Joseph was "doing very well," Leonora was "married last spring," Addie is "with grandparents," and Michael, a "good boy, is in college."[7]

Many children wrote to Sister Irene. "Your little boy, Freddie" wrote: "I got the prize last month for taking the highest per cent in spelling. I am beginning to save my money, and I have 44 cents. Have had a real nice time this winter sliding on my sled. I am well, and so is Mamma. Good-bye. Mamma and I send love to you."[8]

Sister Irene wanted to make sure her foundlings received the same treatment in their new families that they would if they were the same flesh and blood. She also wanted to be able to take a child away from a home that turned out badly. Instead of encouraging adoption, which could mean loss of control, Sister Irene and her successor, Sister Teresa, developed a unique agreement for foster parents. It was called an indenture, but it was very different from the indenture form used by other organizations, which was not much more than a promise of board and keep in exchange for the child's labor until he or she was of age.

The Foundling Hospital's lengthy indenture agreement was filled with safeguards. Many of them were pledges by the foster parents (the "parties of the second part") to treat the child like one of their own.[9]

Foster parents had to agree to provide "all things necessary and fit...and in all respects similar to what would ordinarily be provided and allowed by...one in their station of life, for their own...children."

They had to pledge that the "child shall be maintained, clothed, educated and treated with like care and tenderness as if he were in fact the child of the parties of the second part" and that they would "provide for said child, financially and in every other way, as if the said child were adopted by the said parties of the second part."

They had to promise not to transfer the indenture to anyone else without the consent of the Foundling Hospital...to report on the condition of the child every six months...and to permit visits from representatives of the Foundling Hospital.

Furthermore, foster parents had to agree that, if they should die before the indentured child came of age, the indentured child would be taken care of. It would inherit just as if "said child...had been the natural and legitimate child of the parties of the second part."*

The indenture form for female children had one major difference. That was in the section in which the male child was simply "to be as their own child." Instead of being "as their own child," a girl was to "be employed by said parties of the second part in and about their house and household." There were no provisions as to the tasks a boy was to perform.

This system of indenturing, the sisters believed, "prudently secures to the Institution a control over its wards until they become of age, and it is constantly watchful of their interests."[10] On the Foundling Hospital's 50th anniversary, they announced that "23,301 had been returned to their parents or guardians; 24,658 had been indentured in 'free' homes, and 3,200 had been legally adopted."[11]

Unlike the Children's Aid Society, the Foundling Hospital did not give detailed accounts of how their wards fared in their new homes and what happened to them when they were grown up. It was not until many years later that their stories began to be told.

The complete text of a New York Foundling Hospital indenture form can be found in Appendix A.

Chapter 5

LITTLE WANDERERS AND JUVENILE DELINQUENTS

obody knows for sure how many homeless children, let alone adults, lived in New York City at the time the Foundling Asylum opened its doors. Mr. Brace estimated that there were as many as 30,000 on the city streets. But accurate data, then as now, was hard to come by.

Other cities also had populations of orphaned and homeless children. In Boston there were several child-saving agencies that believed, like Mr. Brace, that foster homes in the country were the best places for such youngsters.

The Boston Children's Mission was dedicated to the "rescue from vice and degradation of morally exposed children of this city." It started sending bands of children to rural New England towns even before the founding of the Children's Aid Society. The mission's orphan train program continued into the 1890s, taking parties of children to midwestern states as well as New England.

Also in Boston was the New England Home for Little Wanderers, founded the year the Civil War ended and still going strong today.

Many of its wards were the orphans of sailors and soldiers who had lost their lives in the war. In its first year the home placed out 178 children. More than half went to families in Massachusetts. The rest went out of state, with the largest group—26—going to Michigan. One child was placed in Canada, and one in California.[1]

An 1889 story in the *Kokomo* (Indiana) *Dispatch* describes the reception of a band of "little wanderers" from Boston:

> Guests who breakfasted early at the Hotel Clinton Sunday morning were more or less startled to see nearly one-half of the big dining room occupied by children, ranging in age from two to twelve years. Their wonder was not decreased when, at a given signal, more than a score of little heads bowed down and as many tiny voices were lifted up in unison in that sweetest and most meaning of prayers—"Give us this day our daily bread."

The article further described how the 24 children were accompanied by the Reverend V. A. Cooper, the superintendent of the New England Home for Little Wanderers; a matron; a missionary agent; and a nurse, "in order that they might be given Christian homes in accordance with the custom of that worthy charitable institution."[2]

One of the two-year-old little wanderers was Mary Blacklidge, whose adoptive parents agreed that Mary would receive "a good Common School Education; attend Church and Sunday School; be cared for in Sickness and Health," and that they would "keep the Home informed of the welfare of the child once in six months."

According to her daughter, Martha, Mary had a wonderful life in a family who provided her with all kinds of advantages. But, in the final illness of her old age, Mary's mind sometimes wandered. She would ask: "Why didn't my mother love me? Why did my mother give me away?"

Martha was astounded by the question. Not knowing that her mother was adopted, Martha kept saying, "But Mom, she did love you!"

Then, in March of 1980, Martha received a phone call from a stranger. It was a woman who was trying to trace some of her relatives.

> She asked me, "Is your mother the Mary Blacklidge who come to Kokomo on an orphan train?"
>
> I said, "Yes, my mother is Mary Blacklidge Wagner. But I don't know what you're talking about when you say 'orphan train.'" After what seemed like a very long pause, she said:
>
> "Oh! Didn't you know your mother is adopted?" Without hesitating, she continued, "Oh, I had better hang up. I'm sorry."
>
> Very anxiously I shouted, "Please, don't you dare hang up!" She proceeded to tell me that her mother, uncle, and aunt had been on the same train with my mother. She was trying to find out what happened to her aunt, and hoped that my mother might be able to shed some light on the mystery.

Thanks to this call, Martha was able to talk to her mother about a portion of her life that had always been hidden. Martha also received permission to try to find out who her mother's *real* mother was.

Mary Blacklidge Wagner died before Martha could unravel the mystery of her mother's origins. She was able to do this through information supplied by the New England Home for Little Wanderers.*

"In answer to mother's questions—'Why did my mother give me away?' and 'Why didn't she love me?'—there, of course, can be many answers," Martha wrote after her mother's death. "But I have to feel that Mary Frances [her mother's biological mother] expressed her

---

*Information about where to write to trace the forebears of orphan train children can be found in
  Appendix B.

Two little wanderers ready for their trip to new homes.

love by the sacrifice of giving mother a beautiful, loving, happy and better life—one she could never have provided for her."[3]

Like the Children's Aid Society, both the Children's Mission and the New England Home for Little Wanderers were closely involved with the Protestant community. But Boston was a city with an exploding population of newly arrived Irish Catholics. So it was hardly surprising that Boston's Home for Destitute Catholic Children decided it should take care of its own with a rural placing-out program. Early in 1865, 48 children destined for homes with New England Catholic farm families boarded the first Catholic orphan train from Boston.

Records of the Home for Destitute Catholic Children indicate that foster children were fairly often sent back to them. An 1866 journal entry notes:

> Mr. Thomas Allen of Marblehead sent by Express the boy James Donlon who was sent to him two years ago; he says the boy is constantly running away and can do nothing with him. It took him a long time to find out.[4]

The Catholic orphan trains from Boston stopped running around the end of the century. They were replaced by streetcars (i.e., trolley cars) in which children were taken on Sunday mornings to churches in the Boston area. Following mass, the "streetcar babies" were put on display to be looked over by prospective foster parents. It was a procedure that some called "the parish slave auction."[5]

In Boston, as in New York, there were also destitute and abandoned black children. But placing out was not a popular option for them. Even when the orphan train movement was at its height, most wound up in poorhouses or the segregated "colored orphanages." In New York, Charles Loring Brace remarked on how few black children came their way during the early years of the Aid Society:

"It is a noticeable thing that during this age of poverty, not a single colored boy has come under the operations of this Society, and only two during the two years of our labors."[6] Once in a long while a black waif would be sent out on an orphan train to be ultimately placed with a black family.

Writing from Iowa ten years after the Civil War, the western agent of the Aid Society told of feeling doubts about placing the one "little colored boy" in the party. Fortunately, he managed to find "a colored pillar of the Baptist church"—a "Mr. T." But Mr. T. was reluctant to come see the boy. Then came another of those happy endings the society loved to recount:

"He took the little fellow in his arms in order to get a better look at him, and no sooner had he done so than Johnny put both his arms around his neck and snuggled up to him with a sense of conscious rest and protection that broke Mr. T. down completely. Turning to me, with his eyes full of tears, he said 'I'll have to keep him.'"[7]

Jewish children were equally rare among the groups sent West. There was only one among those on the train that arrived in Dowagiac, Michigan, in 1854: "a little German Jew," according to the Reverend Mr. Smith, "who had been entirely friendless for four years, and had finally found his way into the Newsboys' Lodging House."[8]

In Boston destitute Jewish children in need were looked after by the Federation of Jewish Charities. From time to time the federation sent Jewish children to the Children's Mission or the New England Home for Little Wanderers for placing out in rural homes.[9] In New York at the century's end, when large numbers of Jews were fleeing the pogroms of czarist Russia, Jewish agencies had more than they could cope with. Most of their homeless children were placed in Jewish orphan asylums. But many found their way to the Aid Society. And Jewish foundlings were sometimes baptized as Catholics and sent West on the baby trains.[10]

There were still other agencies that sent young people to the western states in the second half of the 19th century. Among them were

The Hebrew Orphan Asylum in New York

institutions whose primary aim was to educate and reform juvenile delinquents and potential juvenile delinquents. One of these was the New York City House of Refuge, which turned many of its "graduates" over to the Children's Aid Society for placing out.

The House of Refuge was the first institution for wayward children in the country. Like the almshouses (poorhouses) throughout the country, it had been binding out its wards long before the Aid Society came along. It was founded in the 1820s by the Society for the Reformation of Juvenile Delinquents. This was a group of concerned citizens who believed that jails and penitentiaries were "schools and colleges of crime." In these grim institutions of criminal learning, the young were mingled with the old just as they were in the almshouses. Boys (and sometimes girls) were imprisoned not only for crimes, but also for such vague offenses as vagrancy. All that vagrancy amounted to was having no apparent home and no visible means of support.[11]

Many of the children and teenagers in the House of Refuge were offenders who had been sent there by the courts. But others had no criminal records, only parents who couldn't—or didn't want to—handle them anymore, and felt a little reformation would be good for them. As soon as a young person was deemed sufficiently reformed, he or she was bound out. Some of the boys were bound out as apprentice seamen on whaling and merchant ships; others were sent to work on farms, where they were indentured until they were 21. Girls were indentured as servants until they were 18.[12]

A similar organization, the New York Juvenile Asylum, also sent children West, but in their own orphan trains. Founded in 1851 for the care of vagrant and neglected children, it is still operating today. But now it is called The Children's Village and is located in Dobbs Ferry, about ten miles north of the city.

The aim of the Juvenile Asylum's public-spirited founders was "not the establishment of a Juvenile Prison, or the subjection of unruly children to a merely punitive discipline…but to found an Asylum where the friendless child might find friends, the wayward child might be taught the lessons of self-government, and all coming to it might be placed under kindly home influences."[13]

Like Mr. Brace of the Aid Society, those behind the Juvenile Asylum believed that "the Great West furnished the best field for reform." The asylum's 1860 annual report declared: "We have found by practical experience that in this country agricultural pursuits are the most elevating, and afford the widest field for permanent improvement and success."[14]

At first the asylum turned boys over to the Aid Society for placing out in the West. An early report of the Aid Society notes that, of the children "sent away" from the city in one year, 42 were from the Juvenile Asylum.[15]

But soon the Juvenile Asylum was sending out its own emigrant parties. Clad in brand-new clothes, and in groups of 50 or thereabouts, they often traveled in a private car from the Erie Railroad depot in Jersey City.

Early in April 1879 a notice headed ASYLUM CHILDREN appeared in the *Kankakee* (Illinois) *Gazette:*

> A company of about twenty children from the New York Juvenile Asylum, from seven to twelve years of age, will be at the Commercial Hotel, Kankakee, Wednesday morning April 16, 1879.
>
> Homes are wanted for them with farmer's families in this and adjoining counties, where they will receive kind treatment, good moral training and a fair common school education.
>
> They may be on trial for two weeks and then under indentures, until of age, provided they prove satisfactory.
>
> The terms of the indentures are such that they will receive a common school education and paid one hundred dollars and two suits of clothes when of age.
>
> This company will consist mostly of boys. They will be at the hotel at the appointed time without fail. Please meet them on that day.[16]

Several weeks later the *Kankakee Gazette* ran another story headed ORPHAN CHILDREN. It reported that 19 out of what turned out to be 31 children were "taken by the residents of this city and county."

One of the passengers on the railway car full of orphans and half orphans from the New York Juvenile Asylum was Joseph Grisich, the "poet of Kankakee." Grisich lived in the town where he arrived in 1879 until his death at the age of 99.

At the meeting in the old Commercial Hotel, Joseph was chosen by a farmer from Aroma Park. "I was twelve years old, and my brother Tommy, who went with the Grimes family, was eight. I went to work on the farm for a while, until one day I forgot to do something like water the animals." By then a teenager, and fearful of punishment, he simply "skipped out."

A series of jobs followed: first as a field hand making 50 cents a day, and ultimately as a custodian for the Kankakee Public Schools. Meanwhile, he was constantly writing his poems. In 1921 one of his verses was set to music and became quite a local hit. Ironically for an orphan who could hardly remember his mother, it was called, "Just Drop a Line to Mother" ("because she longs to hear from you, just you").[17]

With the influx of large numbers of children from the city streets in towns throughout the Midwest, some criticism began to be heard. Most of it was directed at the Children's Aid Society, which, in most years, shipped out more children than all the other organizations put together.

The Catholic Protectory of New York faulted the Protestants of the Aid Society for sending out orphans who had not been trained in the "obedience and fidelity" required for family life and accused Mr. Brace and his staff of attempting to root out "every trace of their earlier faith and filial attachment" with the result that "supposed charity turns out to be only sectarian zeal." And one Catholic leader declared, "The system which is flooding our western country with undisciplined, vicious children is much to be deprecated."[18]

The problem of unwanted children in New York City was so great that scarcely a day went by when police did not find an abandoned baby.

Others pointed out that children were handed out too hastily to prospective foster parents, that they weren't checked up on enough once placed, that many were kept home from school in order to work on the farm or do household chores, and that most would be better off in the structured settings of institutions.

The most severe criticism came from people in the states that received the children of the orphan trains. A number of midwesterners claimed that the Aid Society was unloading the offspring of New York's criminal population on their states. Further, they asserted that altogether too many "vicious and depraved children" from the East were ending up in their prisons, reformatories, and almshouses.

The society made several fairly thorough investigations to determine what was really happening. Agents in the states from which most of the criticism came visited almshouses and penal institutions. They reported that the number of Aid Society children who had "gone wrong" was greatly exaggerated.

In 1884 an independent investigator, the secretary of the Minnesota State Board of Corrections and Charities, chided the society for "the hasty placing of children without proper investigation." But he concluded his report by saying:

"Our examination shows, with reference to the children under thirteen years old, that nine-tenths remain, four-fifths are doing well, and all incorrigibles are cared for by the society. If properly placed and faithfully supervised, we are willing to take our full share of these younger children in Minnesota."[19]

From the first, Mr. Brace had been aware that older boys tended to be undependable and were inclined to "skip off" when too much pressure was applied. As for girls between the ages of 14 and 18, "a more difficult class than these to manage, no philanthropic mortal ever came in contact with."[20]

In a letter to the editor of the *New York Tribune,* he responded to the criticism:

We admit, of course, that the large boys change their places, that sometimes a boy is placed in a home where he does not suit the family, or the family him, and in such cases we seek immediately to replace the lad and to make things right in regard to him.

We carry on an immense correspondence with the boys and their Western employers; we hear from the committees who are responsible gentlemen of the place, and our own agents are continually travelling through the States where the children are placed. The agents also employ clergymen or other responsible persons in these villages to visit these children....

As to the stories of ill treatment of our children, whether in the West or South, we hold them to be *bosh.* We should be the first to hear of such cases, and such are scarcely ever reported to us.[21]

There was another cause for criticism that involved something beyond the scope of the Aid Society. By this time many of the midwestern states had big cities. So, too, did the states in the East and South to which the society had been sending children. These cities had orphan and vagrant children of their own to contend with.

The result was that city-based charities in many states started placing-out and binding-out programs for getting children into country homes. Among them were the Children's Aid Society of Indiana, the Children's Home of Cincinnati, and the Children's Home Society of Chicago. Between 1883 and 1909, 28 states set up children's home societies for placing children in families within a state.[22]

Ohio, which had children's homes in almost every county, made certain that children were always placed as far away as possible. This was so that children "were given a start in life far distant from the degrading influence of bad relatives and where no trace of their early history can be found. Even their foster parents are not permitted to know of their previous history." This attitude of secrecy was prevalent for many years in the social work community. It was to make things extremely difficult for those who tried as adults to seek out blood relations.[23]

Homeless children often banded together for safety and company.

Gradually, people were coming around to the view that children were better off in a family setting than in a large institution. As one child care association reported many years later, the orphanages of the time were "huge fortresses, regimented and impersonal, where orphans' heads were shaved for fear of ringworm, life was austere and discipline was stern."[24]

Mr. Brace remained satisfied that his system was the best. It was informal and personal, not regimented and impersonal. It required no legal agreements, which made it preferable to formal indenture. It provided *free* foster homes, with no monetary gain for adults, and that insured better treatment than boarding-out systems where foster parents were paid for caring for their temporary charges.

Mr. Brace could also proudly point to the statistics on the decrease in juvenile crime in New York City since the beginnings of the society—a period in which the city's population had more than doubled. "We are prepared to prove a great diminution of children's crime...not only as proportioned to population, but absolutely."[25]

In his annual reports he would cite an array of statistics about the decrease in the commitments of girls and boys for petty crimes and vagrancy and the decrease in the number of young people arraigned for juvenile delinquency.

But above all Mr. Brace was buoyed up by the many success stories the Children's Aid Society could report.

Chapter 6

ONWARD, UPWARD, AND NOTEWORTHY CAREERS

One spring day in 1859 a band of former street urchins was playing together on a rocky island in New York City's East River. They were running about laughing and shouting when they were interrupted by the appearance of the superintendent of the orphanage where they lived. The boys stopped abruptly, afraid they were about to be scolded.

The superintendent smiled. "Boys," he said, "how would you like to go away and live in the country where you can ride horses and drive cattle?" It seems he had just received a letter from one of their friends, Marty Terrill. Marty had been taken from the island by the Children's Aid Society and sent to Delphi, Indiana. His letter told of the good life that was now his on a farm: animals and apple trees, green fields and great places to swim.

The homeless kids were overjoyed. Before many weeks had passed, they were part of a group of children from The Nurseries bound for Noblesville, Indiana.

The Nurseries, a repository for children four years old and up, consisted of six grim brick buildings. Close by them were the House of Refuge and the Infant Hospital for children under four. (The Infant Hospital was the same one whose high death rate had deeply disturbed the young Charles Loring Brace.)

Two of the boys who had been playing together that spring

day—12-year-old Johnny Brady and 9-year-old Andy Burke—grew up to make their marks in public life. Brady became governor of Alaska; Burke, governor of North Dakota.

A good-looking boy with a sunny disposition, Andy Burke received several offers of a home when he reached Noblesville, Indiana. During the Civil War, he ran away to join the Union army as a drummer boy. After the war the youthful veteran worked his way to Casselton, North Dakota, where he got a job in a bank and became active in Republican politics.[1]

Later, as governor of the state, Andrew Burke wrote a letter of thanks to the Aid Society.

Annette R. Fry

Governor Andrew Burke of North Dakota, one of the many orphan train riders to achieve success

He called forth "God's best blessings" on the agency that had sent him West, and recalled

the long railway ride on the Erie route, the tearful eyes, the saddened hearts, the arrival at Noblesville on that clear, sunshining day, the dread I experienced on awaiting to be selected by one of those who had assembled in the Christian Church at that place, and how my heart was gladdened by Mr. D. W. Butler, for his appearance indicated gentleness. All those scenes will live in memory.[2]

Annette R. Fry

Orphan train rider Henry Jost later became mayor of Kansas City. He is shown here on his arrival in Missouri (left), as a farm hand about nine years later (center), and as mayor (right).

John Green Brady, destined to be appointed governor of the territory of Alaska, had fled his slum home in New York when he was seven. His mother was dead. His father, a longshoreman and heavy drinker, beat him whether he was drunk or sober. The police picked up the runaway boy and took him to the city orphanage.

One of those who had been in Noblesville on the day the train pulled in with its cargo from the East was Judge John Green of Tipton.

"It was the most motley crowd of youngsters I ever did see," the judge was fond of telling in later years. "I decided to take John Brady home with me because I considered him the homeliest, toughest, most unpromising boy in the whole lot. I had a curious desire to see what could be made of such a specimen of humanity." Judge Green lived to see Brady graduate from Yale and Union Theological Seminary. His widow saw her foster son become a three-term Alaska governor.

By a curious coincidence Burke and Brady ran into each other years later in a Kansas City hotel. Ex-governor Brady was then the Alaska delegate to the Trans-Mississippi Congress. Ex-governor Burke was the representative of the Great Western Oil Company. Apparently they spent most of the day talking over old times.[3]

Other states could also tell of boys from the East who became leading citizens—like Congressman (and Judge) James Richards. Richards was taken by the Children's Aid Society to the town of New Philadelphia, Ohio, when he was in his teens.[4] Official biographies make no mention of his having come West in this way. They do, however, mention an unusual claim to fame: He married a female physician![5]

Another successful Aid Society transplant was Thomas Jefferson Cunningham, mayor of Chippewa Falls, Wisconsin, in the 1880s. A prominent figure in Democratic party circles for many years, Cunningham was a friend of three-time presidential candidate William Jennings Bryan. He was also a delegate to 17 national conventions, and in 1940 was the oldest delegate at the convention where Franklin D. Roosevelt was renominated.

Thomas Cunningham apparently never talked about the fact that he came West on a Children's Aid Society train.[6] But the society was well aware of him, as shown by these entries from its 1887 annual report; the first is a copy of a letter replying to a query from New York:

A POOR BOY BECAME MAYOR

Dear Sir:

I have just received the information that you asked me to get for you about the young man sent to Wisconsin through your Society. His name is Thomas C——, Chippewa Falls, Wis., one of the party who went when my brother went. He has been mayor, also a member of the Legislature.

Yours respectively,

F. Osterweld

A copy of page 71. Record 16

Thomas C———. Age 15. Orph. Am. Goes West with Mr. Fry, August 10, 1869. Placed with R. J———, Stoughton, Wis. Wrote to him Jan. 26, 1870.—No reply. Wrote to him Sept., 1870.—No reply. Wrote to him April, 1871.—No reply. Wrote to him Sept., 1871.—No reply. Wrote to him March 12, 1872. In reply, Mr. R. J—— writes (March 26, 1872) that Thomas C—— left him, and went to work in a printing office, where he worked for some time; saw him some time over a year ago. He was working in Boscobel, soliciting orders for cards, etc.

Never heard from him since.[7]

The Children's Aid Society tried its best to keep track of its children. But it wasn't always easy.

Many of the thousands who made good were teenagers who, like Congressman Richards and Mayor Cunningham, simply wanted a free trip to the land of opportunity. Judging by the letters in the society's annual reports, a lot of them appreciated what the society had done for them.

Taken west in 1875, C. J. O'Brien wrote 11 years later from "the finest country in the U.S.":

"When I first came to Kansas, I had an old plug team of horses, and not as much as $5 in my pocket. I took one claim, kept it for about 7 months and sold it for $1,200. I have now got two more claims that I would not take $2,000 for, and have two good mule teams and two cows. Will have calves in the Spring. So you can see I am in better circumstances."[8]

But the homesteading opportunity wasn't all that motivated the westward-bound New Yorkers. Writing from Kansas, Minnie F. explained why it was the best place for girls like her:

"You can save money here, but you can't in New York. I had to work for nearly a year for just my board, and now I can cook, bake, wash and iron, churn, and other work, and am making $2^{1}/$_{2}$ a week, and am living with splendid people, go to Sabbath school and church every Sunday. Mrs. Race says the longer I stay with her the more she will pay me. She thinks I have done wonderfully well."[9]

At the time these letters were written, the frontier in America had all but disappeared; the wilderness had long since been charted, and the bitter struggle with Native Americans for its possession had come to an end with the surrender of Chief Joseph of the Nez Perce in 1877. By the 1890s the best of the "free" land had been latched onto by the homesteaders. But the spirit of enterprise and "git-up-and-go" were far from dead. Americans were convinced that there was nowhere to go but *up.*

Beginning before the Civil War and for many years thereafter, Horatio Alger churned out a stream of novels about boys with "luck and pluck." They always somehow managed to progress from rags to riches. The stories of the Children's Aid Society's successes were immensely appealing to writers like Alger. In *Julius, the Street Boy*, published in the last decade of the century, Alger wrote of an enterprising lad who went West on an orphan train.[10]

Readers loved these stories of slum children who made good. There was a tendency, though, to romanticize not only the successes they achieved, but also the very life they fled from.

St. Nicholas, the nation's most popular magazine for the younger generation, ran a serial called "Teddy and Carrots, Two Merchants of Newspaper Row." In it the life of the boys who lived in packing boxes and other city hideouts is imbued with all the glamour of *Swiss Family Robinson.*[11]

The lives of homeless boys were also described in a nonfiction work, *How the Other Half Lives.* It was a best-selling book of the l890s that created a sensation; its author was Jacob Riis, an immigrant from Denmark, a photographer as well as a journalist and an admirer of

Photos like this one from Jacob Riis's How the Other Half Lives *documented life for the poor in New York's slums.*

Charles Loring Brace. His book described in vivid detail—and with striking pictures—life in New York's slums. His object was to alert the public to the heartbreak and squalor of life among the very poor.

The work of the Aid Society appealed to the well-to-do gentry of the city. Their generous contributions financed the industrial schools, the summer homes by the seashore, the lodging houses for both boys and girls, and hundreds and thousands of railway journeys. The society's emigration work was the pet project of the wealthy Mrs. John

The Bettmann Archive

A photo by Jacob Riis shows young girls working in a tenement shop.

Jacob Astor. Year after year she paid for sending an annual party of 100 children West. And in her will she left $25,000 for that purpose—an amount that would be worth millions today.

For Mr. Brace, who died in 1890, the outward migration of the city children was the great work of what was truly a noteworthy career. (To this day he is regarded as one of the great pioneers of American social work.) In the last year of his life, the society transplanted children—plus a few adults—to 36 states, one territory, Canada, and

Europe, for a total of 2,851 young emigrants. The overall total was not as large as that of the peak year, 1875, when 4,026 were sent out. But it represented the level of a steady flow that would go on for yet another generation.

For many years the society's reports included an account of the "Noteworthy Careers" of those it helped. The last such listing was made in 1917: "a Governor of a State, a Governor of a Territory, two members of Congress, two District Attorneys, two Sheriffs, two Mayors, a Justice of the Supreme Court, four Judges, two college professors, a cashier of an insurance company, twenty-four clergymen, seven high school Principals, two School Superintendents, an Auditor-General of a State, nine members of State Legislatures, two artists, a Senate Clerk, six railroad officials, eighteen journalists, thirty-four bankers, nineteen physicians, thirty-five lawyers, four civil engineers, and any number of business and professional men, clerks, mechanics, farmers, and their wives and others who have acquired property and filled positions of honor and trust."

At the time this list was compiled, Americans were fighting overseas in World War I. The listing concluded, "Nor would the roll call be complete without mention of 7,000 soldiers and sailors in their country's service."[12]

The migration of the New York City children did not stop with the end of the war. One reason it continued was that a devastating epidemic of influenza in 1918 and 1919 left many orphans and half orphans in its wake.

But the days of placing out children in the West and South was dwindling. The society's orphan trains—and the baby trains of the New York Foundling Hospital—kept running for only a few years more.

In 1929 the last orphan train departed from New York City.

Chapter 7

THE LAST
ORPHAN TRAINS

The decline of the orphan trains came about due to a variety of reasons.

One may have been financial: The railroads were no longer providing reduced fares to the eastern charities. In 1906 the Interstate Commerce Commission had cracked down on the railroads for providing free passes and special rates to their friends. Theodore Roosevelt, the "trustbuster," was president, and this was part of the "busting up" of monopolies. The sending of companies of children out of state by both the New York Juvenile Asylum and the New England Home for Little Wanderers stopped about that time.[1]

The main reasons for the decline of the orphan trains were complex. They involved changing attitudes about destitute families and dependent children.

As social work became more professionalized, a new idea took hold. Instead of sending children into strange environments, the emphasis turned to keeping needy families from breaking up. In 1909 the first White House Conference on Children was called by Theodore Roosevelt. It recommended that, wherever possible, children be kept with parents.[2]

"Poverty alone should not disrupt the home," declared President

Roosevelt. "Parents of good character, suffering from temporary misfortune, and above all deserving mothers...deprived of the support of the normal breadwinner, should be given such aid as may be necessary to enable them to maintain suitable homes for the rearing of their children."[3]

New state laws were being passed to help mothers and children. They called for widows' pensions, sickness insurance, compulsory education, and curbs on child labor.

Child labor was now a major issue. Previously, Americans had taken most forms of child labor for granted. When the orphan train movement began, many people thought of children as smaller—and less intelligent—adults whom they could treat as they pleased. In many parts of the country, slavery was an accepted practice. And the indenture of boys and girls was a familiar part of life throughout the nation, and remained so long after the Civil War.

As attitudes about childhood and child labor changed, fewer people were thinking of foster and adopted children as potential workers. It was also becoming more difficult to place older boys. (With improvements in farm machinery, farmers in the Midwest needed fewer hands. Besides, older boys tended to be "troublesome.") There was now much more of a demand—especially from childless couples—for girls and babies for adoption.

To help prepare homeless boys for family life, the Children's Aid Society had started sending them to the 150-acre Brace Memorial Boy's Farm. At the farm—an hour's train ride from the city—they not only were taught how to do outdoor chores, they also became "domesticated." They learned how to eat with a knife and fork, the value of *please* and *thank you,* and habits of personal cleanliness.[4]

In the 1970s one old-timer who was placed on the Brace farm with his younger brother remembered it fondly: "If I could have only stayed ten or twelve years old, I would have stayed there all my life." The training served him well. Gilbert Eadie's schoolboy essay, "How

Gilbert Eadie

Walter (left) and Gilbert (right) Eadie

the Farmer Boy Can Help Win the War," won him a ten-day, all-expenses-paid trip to the Iowa State Fair in 1918. And when his foster parents died, they bequeathed their farm to him.[5]

The stories about orphan train riders like Gilbert Eadie that came to light in the early 1970s almost always told of placing out in midwestern states. But, from the beginning, rural New York State received the greatest number of placed-out children and young adults. Oddly, few of their stories have come to light.

By 1900 the Children's Aid Society was sending increasing numbers to the South, where there was more of a demand for older boys who could work on farms.

In the first two decades of the 20th century, the reports of the Aid Society brimmed with glowing stories of the bigger boys who had done well in states to the South—Texas especially. In the 1905 annual report Robert Brace, the son of the society's founder, described "an undersized boy of sixteen" whom he had taken to Texas nearly five years before

who had run away three times from an orphan asylum, and previous to coming to the Farm School had lived by his wits in the streets. According to his own belief, if left to his own resources he would soon have drifted into the

Boys from New York City work on the farm established by the Children's Aid Society.

life of a criminal. At the Farm School his better instincts were aroused. He proved ready to work and apt to learn.

Now he is as fine and manly a six-foot farmer as one ever meets, has thirty acres of cotton of his own, has good credit in the stores and a good name in the com-

munity, and in a very few years should be a land owner
and a fair type of the class that makes the backbone of
our country.

This case and others that Brace cited "are merely examples of
what our methods have accomplished in hundreds of cases."[6]

Though the numbers were dwindling in the 1920s, groups of
New York City children continued to be sent out by train to states as
far away as Nebraska, Kansas, Missouri, Arkansas, Texas, and
Louisiana.

Because of the many Catholic families there, Louisiana was a
special favorite of the New York Foundling Hospital. But in 1927 the
New York Foundling Hospital officials decided that from then on they
would seek homes for their wards only in New York and neighboring
states.

What was happening was that agencies wanted foster children
where they could check up on them more easily. And adoptions were
becoming carefully supervised transactions, with adoptive parents
matched with children.

Two years after the Foundling Hospital's baby trains stopped
running, the Aid Society announced it was limiting placement of children to within 200 miles of New York City.[7]

An era had come to a close. Charles Loring Brace, Sister Irene,
and the other pioneering child savers were all but forgotten. Few people in America remembered the orphan trains. Most of the many thousands of foundlings, runaways, orphans, and half orphans who had
ridden them seemed intent on burying their pasts.

But, as they grew older, here and there more and more of them
began to wonder. Who were my parents? Where did they come from?
Surely I must have some blood relations, somewhere? And a few of
them began writing to the Aid Society and the Foundling Hospital for
information locked in their files.

Then, in the second half of the 1970s, two events occurred that caused millions of people—including orphan train riders and descendants of orphan train riders—to look proudly into the past that so many of them had turned their backs on.

One was the Bicentennial of the United States—the 200th birthday celebration of the signing of the Declaration of Independence on July 4, 1776.

The other was totally unexpected. It was a television miniseries that brought together an enormous viewing audience throughout the country. For eight consecutive nights in 1977, America watched *Roots,* an epic dramatization of one man's story about his search for his ancestors.

The message of *Roots* was that each of us has a past worth knowing, a past that can help us understand the present. Whoever our forebears were, whether orphans or foundlings, whether native Americans or hyphenated Americans, whether they came to this country in slave ships, or in the steerage of ocean liners, they provide us with our heritage.

Roots was the result of years of genealogical research by writer Alex Haley. His search had taken him back seven generations to his West African forebears. His vivid account of the warrior Kunta Kinte and his descendants made white people as well as black think about their own families and where they came from.

The combination of Haley's findings about his ancestors and the stimulus of the Bicentennial made family research a major activity throughout the country.

An intensive search for the heritage of the orphan train riders was about to begin.

Each year the surviving orphan train riders gather and reenact their trip west as part of the Orphan Train Heritage Society of America's program to remember this period of American history.

Chapter 8

MYSTERIES SOLVED
AND UNSOLVED

**I** am so thankful for God's guiding hand and the Children's Aid Society for sending this little orphan girl to Arkansas to later become my very sweet grandmother."

Charlotte Woodward was telling the story of Carrie Salverson's life for a history of Washington County, Arkansas.

One of the people on the staff of the county history project was Mary Ellen Johnson of Springdale. She listened, fascinated, to Carrie's story. She had never heard of the orphan train movement. She wanted to learn more.

With a little digging and some ads in local papers, Mary Ellen Johnson discovered that there were a surprising number of other families in the area whose lives had been touched by orphans from New York City. Before long her search for information about riders of the orphan trains reached far beyond the boundaries of the Ozark county.

It was the beginning of the Orphan Train Heritage Society of America. Established in 1986, it is today a nationwide organization. It has proved an invaluable clearinghouse of information for the survivors of the placing-out movement and their descendants.[1]

Some 65 years earlier a little three-year-old with the name *Sylvia Wolk* sewn to the hem of her dress arrived in Columbus, Nebraska, on a New York Foundling Hospital baby train. She was picked up at the station by a farm family who already had two small boys, the older their own, the second adopted.

Work was hard, praise sparing, and affection in short supply during Sylvia's childhood. Though she respected her new parents, she often wondered what had happened to her real mother and father. And she also couldn't help but wonder whether she mightn't have some siblings of her own somewhere.

Grown-up and happily married, Sylvia—now Sylvia Wemhoff—embarked on a search for information about her real family. After years of frustration she learned of Mary Ellen Johnson's organization. It was a lucky break for her—and for the Orphan Train Heritage Society as well.

In 1988 "Unsolved Mysteries" was looking for a new kind of mystery to solve. The reenactment of Sylvia Wolk Wemhoff's story on this popular national television program produced an immediate response. From the moment the program ended, the telephones at the Orphan Train Heritage Society began to ring. They continued to ring day and night for the next few weeks.

Orphan train riders and their kin from all over the country had their own mysteries to solve.

But it wasn't until a rebroadcast months later that Sylvia's long search ended. Thanks to "Unsolved Mysteries," Joseph Wolk, Sylvia's older brother, finally learned of the sister he always suspected he had. After 70 years the brother and sister at last were reunited.[2]

As the word about the Orphan Train Heritage Society spread, new stories about the experiences of orphan train riders poured in—stories told by the children themselves, stories told by their children, stories told by their children's children. They told of events seldom described, facts long hidden, pain suppressed. They told tales of courage, compassion, and—occasionally—mistreatment.

There is an amazing lack of bitterness among those who didn't find the best of homes. They survived, and they are proud of it. They are also grateful for what they have been able to accomplish in life. And they get real satisfaction from their children, grandchildren, and—in some cases—great- and great-great-grandchildren. Again and again even those who were mistreated report happy childhood memories.

A boy who ended up doing the work of "three hired men," was to look back on many who were kind to him, and "how beautiful God's world looked on those clear, still nights with a foot of pure white snow on the ground...a great full moon...and a chorus of singing coyotes."[3]

And a child who was whipped repeatedly in one home, and molested in another, was to become the oldest surviving orphan train rider—and proud of it. She was able to look back and say: "I gave my children all the love and affection I never got....Sometimes I wonder how I ever made it, but God was always on my side. I know the Good Lord has things for me to do yet, so I plan on being around a while."[4]

The search for roots continues to be a major preoccupation of those who share the heritage of the orphan trains. *Who* were the parents whose children made those journeys into the unknown? *Where* did they come from? If they were still alive at the time, *why* did they give up their child or children? The "why" question has been especially hurtful.

"Why did you leave me? I miss you so much! Why hasn't anyone in our family come to visit us?" One man remembers imagining talking to his mother as he lay in his bed in the orphanage.[5]

The search for family information usually begins with tracking down a birth certificate. That's not an easy job when real names are hard to come by. To make things even more difficult, the records of some agencies seem to have disappeared off the face of the earth. This is particularly true of orphan asylums, many of which closed down long ago.

Sometimes persistent digging unearths unexpected information, as in the case of Anne Harrison.

Anne was adopted when a toddler by a Catholic couple in

Colorado. They gave her a good home. In her 20s she discovered quite by chance that she was adopted. She also learned that she had been a ward of the New York Foundling Hospital. But her search for a birth certificate did not bring results until many years later and some frustrating dead ends. All she could get from the Foundling Hospital was a baptismal certificate with the names of her adoptive parents in Colorado, plus the news that she had been called Mabel Ryan. When she finally received her birth certificate from the city of New York, she was amazed to learn:

"My name is Mabel Rubin. My mother's name was Jennie Rubin, age 19,

Anne Harrison

Anne Harrison, one of the many orphan train riders who later discovered surprising facts about her family history

born in Russia. My father's name was Moe Cohen, age 21, born in New York City....Obviously, with names like that, my heritage had to be Jewish. *Not to worry! I got the best of both Testaments.*"[6]

A complete history of the orphan train movement has yet to be written and probably never will. Unsolved mysteries there will always be. In many families in America's Midwest, there are ancestors who seem to appear out of nowhere. Some of them could have arrived with the groups of youngsters from the cities. But the clues are few and far between.

As the 20th century draws to a close, the collective descendants of the orphan train riders probably number in the millions. Hundreds of orphan train children are still alive. Many of them have yet to tell their stories. Some of them want to forget the past and never will tell what happened to them.

But those who have told their stories through the Orphan Train Heritage Society have found it gratifying. A woman who came out to Kansas in 1929—the year of the last orphan trains—put it this way:

"On the whole we're the kind of people who don't cry much. But at our reunions everyone cries. It's such a relief to talk to others who understand. We're all a big family. Not by blood, but by something greater. Everyone had a different kind of life, but everyone had the same loss."[7]

For three-quarters of a century the orphan train system served America well. It was an imaginative solution to the problems of destitute and orphaned children at a time when new immigrants were pouring into a country they saw as the new promised land. More than 200,000 children and young people were given a chance to better themselves—a chance unobtainable on city streets or in orphanages and reform schools.[8]

The child savers of the 19th century who fostered this unique migration helped focus attention on the needs of all children. Of course, it was a different America then—a land of farms and small towns—while today's America is dramatically changed.

But what hasn't changed is that many, many children are still at risk.

And what hasn't changed is that today's needy children have problems—some new, some age-old—that also call for creative solutions by people of courage and compassion.

★ ★ ★

NOTES

Chapter 1

1. David J. Rothman, "Our Brothers' Keepers," *American Heritage* 24 (December 1972): 42. The quote is from a "committee conducting a statewide survey in New York" in 1857.

2. "During the last twenty years, a tide of population has settled towards those shores, to which there is no movement parallel in history. During the year 1852 alone, 300,992 alien passengers have landed in New York, or nearly at the rate of *one thousand a day for every week day.* Of these 181,131 were from Ireland, and 118,611 from Germany." Children's Aid Society, *First Annual Report* (1854), 3–4.

3. John William Leonard, *History of the City of New York 1609–1909* (New York: Journal of Commerce and Commercial Bulletin, 1910), 539. According to Leonard, "The population of New York City in 1850 was, by Federal census, 515,477, and in 1860, 805,658." The 10,000 figure is given in Children's Aid Society, *First Annual Report* (New York, 1854), 4.

4. George W. Matsell, chief of police in the New York City Police Department, *Semi-Annual Report, May 31–October 31, 1849* (New York, 1849), Appendix. This is from an excerpt in Robert H. Bremner, ed., *Children & Youth in America*, vol. 1 (Cambridge, Mass.: Harvard Univ. Press, 1972), 755.

5. Children's Aid Society, *First Annual Report* (1854), 5.

Chapter 2

1. Charles Loring Brace, *The Dangerous Classes of New York and Twenty Years' Work among Them*, 3rd ed. (New York: Wyncoop & Hallenbeck, 1880), 54–55.

2. Ibid., 77–78.

3. Ibid., 78–79.

4. Ibid., 236.

5. Ibid., 92.

6. Ibid., 397.

7. Ibid., 88–89.

8. Bremner, vol. 1, 595.

9. Charles Loring Brace, 225.

10. Children's Aid Society, *First Annual Report* (1854), 9.

11. Emma Brace, *The Life of Charles Loring Brace* (New York: Scribner's, 1894), 489–501.

Chapter 3

1. Charles Loring Brace, 320–321.

2. Children's Aid Society, *Second Annual Report* (New York, 1855), 16.

3. Charles Loring Brace, 231–232.

4. Children's Aid Society, *Twenty-third Annual Report* (New York, 1875), 13–14, 59.

5. Children's Aid Society annual reports for 1860s and 1870s.

6. Children's Aid Society, *Ninth Annual Report* (New York, 1862), 43–44.

7. Children's Aid Society, *Tenth Annual Report* (New York, 1863), 75.

8. This information was repeated in Children's Aid Society annual reports in the years following the Civil War.

9. Children's Aid Society, *Eighteenth Annual Report* (New York, 1870), 53–54.

10. Ibid., 58.

11. Children's Aid Society, *Seventeenth Annual Report* (New York, 1869), 62–63.

12. Ibid., 63–64.

13. Howard Zinn, *A People's History of the U.S.* (New York: Harper & Row, 1980), 235–238.

Chapter 4

1. Peggy Deane Toffier Bounder, "Milton Peter Toffier," *Crossroads* 4 (Summer 1988) : 7. (*Crossroads* is a publication of the Orphan Train Heritage Society of America.)

2. Sister Marie de Lourdes Walsh, *The Sisters of Charity of New York*, 1809–1959, vol. 3 (New York: Fordham Univ. Press, 1960), 80.

3. Ibid., 73.

4. Ibid., 17, quoting "the great social reformer of the late 19th century, Elbridge Gerry" at the New York State Constitutional Convention of 1894.

5. Helen Stuart Campbell, *Darkness and Daylight, or Lights and Shadows of New York Life* (Hartford, Conn., 1895), 389–390.

6. *Report of the New York Foundling Hospital, (1898)*. New York, 1990. (Hereafter referred to as *Foundling Hospital Report* with date of year of publication.)

7. *Foundling Hospital Report (1901)*, 16.

8. Campbell, 391; Walsh, 83.

9. Indenture courtesy of Orphan Train Heritage Society of America, Johnson, AR.

10. *Foundling Hospital Report (1890–1901)*, 9.

11. Walsh, 82.

Chapter 5

1. Roberta Star Hirshson, *"There's Always Someone There…": The History of the New England Home for Little Wanderers* (Boston: New England Home for Little Wanderers, 1989), 43.

2. "Homes for the Waifs," *Kokomo Dispatch*, Oct. 17, 1889.

3. Mary Ellen Johnson and Kay B. Hall, *Orphan Train Riders*, vol. 1 (Baltimore: Gateway Press, 1992), 43–51.

4. Peter C. Holloran, *Boston's Wayward Children* (Cranbury, New Jersey: Fairleigh Dickinson Univ. Press, 1992), 97.

5. Ibid., 103.

6. Children's Aid Society, *Second Annual Report* (1855), 16.

7. Children's Aid Society, *Twenty-third Annual Report* (1875), 59.

8. Charles Loring Brace, 246.

9. Holloran, 169.

10. Peter Romanofsky, "To Save Their Souls: The Care of Dependent Jewish Children in New York City, 1900–05," *Jewish Social Studies* 36 (July–Oct. 1974), 253–261.

11. Joseph M. Hawes, *Children in Urban Society: Juvenile Delinquency in Nineteenth-Century America* (New York: Oxford Univ. Press, 1971), 27, 34–36.

12. Bremner, vol. 1, 672.

13. Ibid., 737.

14. New York Juvenile Asylum, *Eighth Annual Report* (New York, 1860), 35–36.

15. Children's Aid Society, *Second Annual Report* (1855), 6.

16. *Kankakee Gazette*, Apr. 3, 1879.

17. "Man, 95, Offers Some Advice," *Kankakee Daily Journal*, Aug. 22, 1963.

18. Quotes are from Miriam Z. Langsam, *Children West* (Madison: Univ. of Wisconsin Press, 1964), 48–49; Bremner, vol. 1, 749.

19. Bremner, vol. 2, 309–312; Langsam, 57–62; Secretary and Agents of the Children's Aid Society, *New York Homeless Children Sent to the West and the National Conference of Charities* (New York, 1883), passim; Rev. Hastings H. Hart, "Placing Out Children in the West," reprint from *The Proceedings of the Eleventh Annual Conference of Charities and Correction* (Boston, 1885).

20. Charles Loring Brace, 307.

21. Reprint of letter to the editor, *New York Tribune*, Mar. 14, 1883, in *New York Homeless Children Sent to the West*, 7–8.

22. Marilyn Irvin Holt, *The Orphan Trains: Placing Out in America* (Lincoln, Neb.: Univ. of Nebraska Press, 1992), 115; Bremner, vol. 2, 317.

23. National Conference of Charities and Correction, *History of Child Saving in the United States* (1892; reprint, Montclair, New Jersey: Patterson Smith, 1971), 134.

24. Jewish Child Care Association of New York, *70,000 Children: How We Cared—Then and Now* (New York, 1972), unpaginated.

25. Children's Aid Society, *Twenty-third Annual Report* (New York, 1885), 6.

Chapter 6

1. *Indianapolis Sunday Star*, Dec. 9, 1906, Magazine section; James D. McCabe, Jr., *Lights and Shadows of New York Life; or the Sights and Sensations of the Great City* (Philadelphia, 1872; reprint, New York: Farrar, Straus & Giroux, 1970), 631–647.

2. Children's Aid Society, *Thirty-ninth Annual Report* (New York, 1891), 18.

3. *Indianapolis Star*, Dec. 9, 1906.

4. Children's Aid Society, *Forty-fourth Annual Report* (New York, 1896), 76–77.

5. *History of Tuscarawas County, Ohio* (Chicago, 1884), 716.

6. Obituary, *Madison* (WI) *Capital Times*, Apr. 28, 1941. There's no mention of how he got west in this obit., and a letter to me from Cunningham's granddaughter, Mary Parks Rafter, Mar. 24, 1972, says that his family knew nothing about the Children's Aid Society.

7. Children's Aid Society, *Thirty-fifth Annual Report* (New York, 1887), 75.

8. Children's Aid Society, *Thirty-fourth Annual Report* (New York, 1886), 76.

9. Ibid., 77.

10. Holt, 18.

11. James Otis, "Teddy and Carrots, Two Merchants of Newspaper Row," *St. Nicholas Magazine* vol. 22 (beginning May 1895).

12. Children's Aid Society, *Sixty-fifth Annual Report* (New York, 1917), 12–13.

Chapter 7

1. Hirshson, 44; Holt, 105; Carol Pugh, director of alumni affairs, Children's Village, Nov. 11, 1992, telephone conversation.

2. Bremner, vol. 2, "Care of Children in Their Own Homes," 365.

3. Rothman, 101.

4. Children's Aid Society, *Sixty-seventh Annual Report* (New York, 1919), 11.

5. Eadie's story is contained in correspondence with writer now at Iowa State Dept. of History and Archives. Also *Cedar Rapids Gazette*, Dec. 25, 1988.

6. Children's Aid Society, *Fifty-third Annual Report* (New York, 1905), 33–34.

7. Walsh, 93; letter from Elizabeth A. Stringer, Director, Foster Care Services, Children's Aid Society, June 29, 1972.

Chapter 8

1. Charlotte Woodward in Johnson and Hall, vol. 1, 305; telephone conversations with Charlotte Woodward, March 1993.

2. Sylvia Wolk Wemhoff in Johnson and Hall, 363–370; telephone conversations Feb. 18 and March 6, 1993.

3. Landkamer in Johnson and Hall, 405.

4. Marguerite Thomson, talk at reunion of Orphan Train Heritage Society, Fayetteville, AR, Oct. 24, 1992; Johnson and Hall, 246.

5. William E. Oser in Johnson and Hall, 383.

6. Anne Harrison in Johnson and Hall, 197–202.

7. Alice Bullis Ayler in "In Search of the Orphan Train Riders," Christine Schultz, *Old Farmers' Almanac 1993*, No. 201 (Dublin, New Hampshire, 1992), 102. We know from newspaper articles, and from stories like Mrs. Ayler's, that the Children's Aid Society sent groups of children to both Kansas and Missouri in 1929. However, the Children's Aid Society no longer has the records of when groups were sent out for public distribution in the course of a year and to which towns. In January 1930 the Board of Trustees confirmed that they were now limiting "the placement of children in permanent homes to a distance of two hundred miles from New York City except within the boundaries of New York State." (Letter from Director of Foster Care Services to writer, June 29, 1972.)

8. There's no agreement about numbers sent out. Records such as there are are contradictory. In 1972 the Children's Aid Society suggested "around" or "not more than" 100,000. Most people today will come up with a ballpark figure of "more than 150,000" for all the agencies. The jacket of Marilyn Holt's definitive 1992 book, *The Orphan Trains: Placing Out in America*, states, "Between 1853 and 1929 at least 200,000 children and several thousand adults participated in a migration unique in America's history."

APPENDIX A

COPY OF NEW YORK FOUNDLING HOSPITAL INDENTURE FOR MALE CHILD

(Note: The underlined material represents handwritten entries in blank spaces provided on form.)

THIS INDENTURE, made this <u>25</u> day of <u>Feb</u> in the year of Our Lord One Thousand Nine Hundred and <u>eleven</u> between THE NEW YORK FOUNDLING HOSPITAL, a Corporation incorporated and organized under the Laws of the State of New York, party of the first part, and <u>Ariane Locier [or Louer]</u> and <u>Amelia</u>, his wife, of <u>Opelousas</u>, State of <u>La</u>, parties of the second part:

WHEREAS, <u>Fred Salentel</u>, male child now of the age of <u>six</u> years and <u>one</u> months, was heretofore, pursuant to the provisions of the Charter of the aforesaid Corporation, received and taken, and now is under its care and custody, and has now, in the judgment of its Board of Managers, arrived at a suitable age for the said Corporation to indenture.

NOW, THEREFORE, this Indenture WITNESSETH, that the said party of the first part, in and by virtue of the power and authority conferred upon and possessed by it, under and by chapter three hundred and nineteen of the Laws of the State of New York for the year 1848, chapter six hundred and thirty-five of the Laws of said State for the year 1872, and chapter nineteen of the Laws of said State for the year 1909, being chapter fourteen of the Consolidated Laws known as the Domestic Relations Law, do hereby put, place, and indenture the said <u>Fred Salentel</u> unto the said par<u>ties</u> of the second part, as <u>their</u> own child in every respect, until the said <u>Fred Salentel</u> shall arrive at the age of Twenty-one years to live with, and be as <u>their</u> own child, during all of which time the said male child shall live with and obey said par<u>ties</u> of the second part, and according to his power, will and ability shall honestly, orderly and obediently in all things demean and behave himself toward the par<u>ties</u> of the second part.

The par<u>ties</u> of the second part agree as follows:

I.—That during all the time aforesaid <u>Ariane & Amelia Louer</u> will provide said <u>Fred Salentel</u> with suitable and proper board, lodging and medical attendance, and all things necessary and fit for any indentured child, and in all respects similar to what would ordinarily be provided and allowed by the said par<u>ties</u> of the second part, or one in <u>their</u> station of life, for <u>their</u> own child or children.

If the said child is returned to the party of the first part when he shall become Twenty-one years of age, then the par<u>ties</u> of the second part will give to said child a new Bible, a complete suit of new clothes, together with all those he shall then have in use, and an outfit of at least <u>the same as their own children in every respect</u>. [This last was written into a blank space provided for a sum of money: "_____dollars"; the word "dollars" being crossed out.]

II.—That the said par<u>ties</u> of the second part will teach and instruct, or cause to be taught or instructed, said child in all branches of education ordinarily taught to the children of persons in the station of life of the said par<u>ties</u> of the second part, such being the ordinary branches of school education and such as are required by law, including, reading, writing and the general rules of arithmetic, and will bring him up in a moral and correct manner, and in the Catholic faith, and cause and procure said child to behave himself in all things as all minor children should demean themselves during their minority, and generally that said child shall be maintained, clothed, educated and treated with like care and tenderness as if he were in fact the child of the par<u>tie</u>s of the second part, and will provide for said child, financially and in every other way, as if the said child were adopted by the said par<u>tie</u>s of the second part under the laws of the State of New York.

III.—That the said par<u>tie</u>s of the second part will not, nor will <u>their</u> legal representatives or assigns, assign or transfer this Indenture to any other person without the consent in writing of the party of the first part.

IV.—That the said par<u>tie</u>s of the second part will, at least once in every six months during said term, report in writing to the Board of Managers of the said party of the first part, or the Treasurer thereof, the conduct or behaviour of said child, and whether said child is still living under the care of the par<u>tie</u>s of the second part, and if not, where and with whom said child is living, and will in such case further state why said child is not living with <u>them</u> and under <u>their</u> care and protection; but neither such report nor its receipt or acceptance by the party of the first part shall be deemed a consent to an assignment of this Indenture or a waiver of any forfeiture thereof.

V.—That the Offices and Managers of the said party of the first part may from time to time visit and see such child, and ascertain to their own satisfaction whether such par<u>tie</u>s of the second part <u>are</u> fully carrying out and performing all the conditions of this Indenture, and whether said child is in all respects properly cared for.

VI.—And it is further provided that this present Indenture shall not be construed to render the said party of the first part responsible in damages for any cause whatever, but shall operate only as the full exercise of the powers conferred by its Charter or Act of Incorporation for the purposes herein expressed.

VII.—And it is hereby mutually agreed by and between the parties hereto, that in case of any breach by said parties of the second part, of the stipulations, agreements or covenants herein contained, set forth and implied, then this Indenture, and each and every part thereof, shall, at the option of the said party of the first part, be null and void, and that the waiver of one breach or forfeiture shall not operate as a general waiver, but only and exclusively of the breach or forfeiture thus waived.

VIII.—And the parties of the second part further agree that, if said child be not returned to the party of the first part when he attains the age of Twenty-One years, or shall have been so returned before he shall have attained such age, then the parties of the second part, in consideration of this Indenture and of being permitted by the party of the first part to keep such child, shall be deemed to have elected to keep, treat and maintain such child as if it were their own natural and legitimate child. And the parties of the second part further agree that, if the parties of the second part shall die intestate, said child shall inherit and succeed to such share of the property, real and personal, of which the parties die seized and possessed, as would have descended or would have been distributed to said child if he had been the natural and legitimate child of the parties of the second part; and that if the parties of the second part shall die leaving a last will and testament, such will shall contain a provision or provisions, giving, bequeathing and devising to said child at least as large a share of the estate, real and personal, of the testator, as he would have received if said testator had died intestate and said child had been the natural and legitimate child of the parties of the second part.

IN WITNESS WHEREOF, the said party of the first part has hereunto caused its corporate seal to be affixed and this Indenture to be signed by its Treasurer, and the said parties of the second part have hereunto set their hand and seal, the day and year first above written.

Sister Teresa Vincent
Treasurer

APPENDIX B

WHERE TO WRITE FOR INFORMATION ABOUT ORPHAN TRAIN RIDERS

Children's Aid Society
Office of Closed Records
150 East 45th Street
New York, NY 10017

Children's Village
(Formerly New York Juvenile Asylum)
Office of Alumni Affairs
Dobbs Ferry, NY 10522

New York Foundling Hospital
Department of Closed Records
590 Avenue of the Americas
New York, NY 10001

Orphan Train Heritage Society of America (OTHSA)
P.O. Box 496
Johnson, AR 72741-0496
(501) 756-2780

FOR FURTHER READING

Nonfiction

Brace, Charles Loring. *The Dangerous Classes of New York and Twenty Years' Work among Them.* New York: 1880. Reprint, New Jersey: Patterson Smith, 1967.

Children's Aid Society. *Annual Reports 1–10.* New York: 1854–1863. Reprint, Arno Press and *New York Times,* 1971 (now handled by Ayer Company Publishers, Salem, New Hampshire).

Fry, Annette Riley. "The Children's Migration." *American Heritage,* December 1974, 4–10.

Holt, Marilyn Irvin. *The Orphan Trains: Placing Out in America.* Lincoln, Neb.: University of Nebraska Press, 1992.

Jackson, Donald Dale. "It Took Trains to Put Street Kids on the Right Track Out of the Slums." *Smithsonian,* August 1986, 95–103.

Johnson, Mary Ellen, and Kay B. Hall. *Orphan Train Riders, Their Own Stories.* Vols. 1 and 2. Baltimore: Gateway Press, 1992, 1993.

Wheeler, Leslie. "The Orphan Trains," *American History Illustrated,* December 1983, 10–23.

Fiction

De Vries, David. *Home at Last.* New York: Dell, 1990.

Holland, Isabelle. *The Journey Home.* New York: Scholastic, 1990.

Nixon, Joan. *The Orphan Train Quartet: A Family Apart, Caught in the Act, In the Face of Danger, A Place to Belong.* New York: Bantam Books, 1988–1990.

Peart, Jane. *Orphan Train West Trilogy: Homeward the Seeking Heart, Quest for Lasting Love, Dreams of a Longing Heart.* Tarrytown, New York: Fleming H. Revell Co., 1990.

Petrie, Dorothea G., and James Magnuson. *Orphan Train.* New York: Dial Press, 1978.

Talbot, Charlene Joy. *An Orphan for Nebraska.* New York: Atheneum, 1979.

INDEX

L
Louisiana, 36, 76

M
Massachusetts, 46, 47
Michigan, 19-21, 47, 51
Minnesota, 57
Minnesota State Board of Corrections and
    Charities, 57
Missouri, 26, 32, 64, 76

N
Nebraska, 76, 80
New England, 46, 50
New England Home for Little Wanderers,
    46-51, 72
New York (state), 20, 32, 74
New York City, 6, 9-21, 24, 25, 29, 31-36, 40,
    46, 50, 51, 60, 64-70, 75, 76, 80
  Blackwells (Roosevelt) Island, 12
  East River, 25, 62
  Five Points district, 12
  Lower East Side, 12, 13
  population of, 60
  slums of, 9, 12, 19, 28, 31, 67
    overcrowding in, 10, 15, 18
    unsanitary conditions in, 9, 19
  street gangs of, 10
  tenements of, 12, 13
New York City House of Refuge, 52, 53, 62
New York Foundling Hospital, 70, 76, 80, 83
New York Infant Hospital, 62
New York Juvenile Asylum, 53, 54, 72
New York Tribune, 57
newsboys, 10, 16, 17, 25, 29, 30, 51
North Dakota, 63
Norwegians, 20, 31
Nurseries, The, 62

O
Ohio, 31, 58, 65
orphan trains, 19, 20-24, 27, 28, 30, 31, 34, 36-44,
    47, 50, 51, 53, 54, 55-57, 62-66, 69-84, 93
  decline of, 72
  peak of, 70
Orphan Train Heritage Society of America,
    78-81, 84
orphanages, 59, 62, 64, 82, 84
orphans
  adoption of, 18, 27, 40, 43, 48, 73, 76, 81, 83
  black, 50, 51
  descendants of, 77, 80-84
  indenture of, 18, 43, 44, 53, 54, 60, 73
    transfer of, 44
  length of working day for, 18
  treatment of, 43, 53, 54, 58, 60, 73, 81, 82
  wages of, 18
outdoor relief, 8

P
Pennsylvania, 25, 40
placing out, 50, 58, 74
poorhouses, 9, 18, 50, 52, 53, 57
poverty, 15, 31, 40, 50, 68, 72
prisons, 14, 19, 53, 57
prostitution, 10, 12
Protestants, 50, 55

R
railroads, 34, 54, 68, 72
reform schools, 14, 84
Riis, Jacob, 67-68
Roosevelt, Franklin D., 65
Roosevelt, Theodore, 72-73
Roots, 77

S
scarlet fever, 39
smallpox, 39
Smith, E. P., 20-21, 51
Society for the Reformation of Juvenile
    Delinquents, 53
"street arabs," 10, 25
"street rats," 20
"streetcar babies," 50
Supreme Court, 70

T
Texas, 74-76
tuberculosis, 9, 25

U
United States, Bicentennial of, 77
"Unsolved Mysteries," 81

V
vagrancy (see homelessness)

W
wet nurses, 37
White House Conference on Children, 72
Wisconsin, 21, 43, 65
workhouses, 9
World War I, 70

Y
yellow fever, 9